Portraits of Steam

The Paintings and Photographs of George F. Heiron

Portraits of Steam

The Paintings and Photographs of George F. Heiron

GEORGE F. HEIRON with MICHAEL HARRIS

Oxford Publishing Co

Half title:
'Battle of Britain' Pacific No 34069 *Hawkinge* climbs the fearsome gradients up the Slade Valley to Mortehoe
with the Ilfracombe-Waterloo through coaches of the 'Atlantic Coast Express', May 1963.

Title page:
No 5018 *St Mawes Castle* rattles the windows of the signalbox at Frampton Crossing as it blasts up the 1 in 60
to Sapperton with the 11.30am Cheltenham St James-Paddington express on 3 October 1953.

Above:
The express from Newcastle on Tyne due at Bristol Temple Meads at 8.20pm makes the Mangotsfield stop
(connection for Bath Green Park) in the late 1950s. Its engine is a BR Standard '5' 4-6-0.
GH: **This was taken from the top of a cliff. I set the camera up on a tripod and a friend who had come along with**
me flashed the gun. The only problem was the glow from the firedoor.

First published 2000

ISBN 0 86093 554 X

© Ian Allan Publishing 2000

Published by Oxford Publishing Co

an imprint of Ian Allan Publishing Ltd, Terminal House, Shepperton, Surrey
TW17 8AS.
Printed by Ian Allan Printing Ltd, Riverdene Business Park, Hersham, Surrey,
KT12 4RG.

Code: 0011/A2

Contents

A fine view of No 4097 *Kenilworth Castle* as it was heading west near Brinkworth on the South Wales line.

The engine crew of 'Britannia' Pacific No 70045 *Lord Rowallan* maintain a sharp look-out (as the railway rule-books demanded) as the summer Saturday train they are working makes its approach to Bristol Temple Meads in 1965, by which time steam was coming near the end of its time in the city.
GH: The engine was painted in unlined green and the crew looked just right!

Foreword
by Ian Allan

George Heiron, artist, at work.

It seems that George Heiron has been around forever, but when I think back it must have been around 1960 when his artistry began to become well-known and appreciated. Until then Vic Welch had been predominant in railway paintings though he was more a locomotive man than a purveyor of the general scene.

Until I visited George at his home in Coalpit Heath I had not realised what a character he is. Clambering up the stairs to see his magnificent model railway which occupied the whole of the roof space I espied a photograph of George at the top of the Matterhorn and made some flippant remark about clever trick photography or superimposing his likeness on the famous mountain. But, I was assured, no tricks this was a genuine photograph taken 12,000 feet up in the air, for George is a skillful and experienced mountaineer as well as being a top notch artist and photographer.

For almost 50 years George has put his talent to good use and scores of pictures, mostly of trains, have emanated from his hand, though other commissions of all sorts have been executed and now we are able to reproduce this magnificent collection of his later works which compliment the illustrations in his earlier book *The Majesty of British Steam* which was published in 1973. I am proud to be associated with the publication of this remarkable collection and valuable works of art found in private collections as well as those which which now adorn the walls of our offices in Shepperton and Hersham.

George can write this caption better than anyone else:
Happy days! In the 1950s when country lanes were traffic-free (and free of associated litter), banks and hedgerows
were sweet with wild flowers and glow-worms by night. Ladies were attractive and charming like 18-year-old
Shirley Tanner of Westerleigh, watching the 8am Neyland-Paddington express passing Westerleigh Junction one
June morning in 1957.

Introduction

Most of us cherish a close identification with our place of birth; it's a way of defining who we are. Anyone meeting George Heiron for the first time, or knowing of his work as an artist or photographer, would have no doubt of his affection for and interest in the city of Bristol — the city of Cabot, the Merchant Venturers, Brunel and the Great Western Railway. For most of his life George has lived in or near Bristol and some of the city's themes run through his work as Blackpool runs through a stick of rock. George has always said that he comes from the middle of that network known as the 'railway crossroads of the west'.

To a generation or so of people interested in railways George's work has probably conditioned their impression of Bristol and its railways. Travelling by train along our rationalised railway network, mention of St Anne's Park, Stoke Gifford or Chipping Sodbury conjures up a study of a steam age express photographed by George — a briskly working Great Western 'Castle' or 'King' taking a 'proper' train of gleaming coaches past a manicured cutting or lineside. The reality of today, in which a one- or two-coach diesel train makes its mundane way through cuttings shaggy with overgrowth or past bridges disfigured with graffiti, comes as something of an anti-climax.

This marks out George's contribution to the world of railways: the images he thought were important and worth capturing not only attracted our attention at the time of their publication but have become imprinted in our consciousness. I understood both his craft and his skill when I accompanied him and his wife, Shirley, on a car tour of once favoured steam age locations for photography. More to say later about this fascinating trip down memory lane.

There is no doubting his fascination with railways. His mother took him to Bristol Temple Meads station to see the pride of the Great Western Railway, No 6000 *King George V*. He remembers hearing the engine's buffer beam mounted bell tolling, as it did in prewar years. This is an early memory, from the start of the 1930s. There was a strange irony, for, in the final months of the GWR, my mother wheeled me in my push-chair to Paddington station, there to see No 6000. Divided by sixteen or so years, two toddlers began their lifelong interest in railways, inspired by the same locomotive but at different ends of the same main line.

As a National Serviceman, George was posted to the Suez Canal Zone, Egypt. There he took photographs of the same engines that, as a schoolboy, I vividly remember crossing over the bridge that spanned one of Ismailia's main streets. Twice in our lives we were touched by the same experiences and, respectfully, I believe it has helped to give me an insight into George's outlook and enthusiasms.

Of the railway photographers and artists of the steam age, they were either one or the other. Treacy was always the photographer, Hamilton Ellis was the painter of the Trains We Loved.

So George Heiron is arguably unique — imaginative and thoroughly competent both as photographer and artist — someone who has used his expertise with one skill to reinforce the other. For this reason, his contribution to the interest in railways is important as many of our younger contemporary railway artists never actually saw the trains that feature in their work. George has based much of the detail — of the lineside, the track, the railway workers, and above all the locomotives and the rolling stock — on his first-hand knowledge of what everything looked like in the Indian summer of the steam age. That is the difference that distinguishes his work.

This book is the first time that the complete photographer and artist has made his appearance. Although George's paintings and photographs have appeared many times in print and he has been commissioned to produce a number of books in which they have featured, until now they have never come together in one volume to demonstrate his overall contribution to our enjoyment and interest.

In conclusion, I would like to record my thanks to George and Shirley Heiron for welcoming me into their home, giving me their time and hospitality, and for letting me share their memories and enthusiasms.

Michael Harris
Ottershaw
Surrey
July 2000

Acknowledgements

In addition to producing numerous paintings for Ian Allan Publishing, George Heiron has undertaken a series of commissions for Brian Stephenson, publisher of *Locomotives Illustrated*. The magazine is published bi-monthly by RAS Publishing, and has now run to over 135 issues each featuring one class or family of British railway locomotives.

George has also produced numerous private commissions and one of his greatest patrons must be Barrie Meikle who asked him in 1987 to paint an LMS 'Princess Coronation'. During the intervening years some 30 or so oil and water colour paintings have been produced and these now adorn Barrie's walls at home.

George and Barrie share a passion for trains as well as the landscape and walking in the lovely Peak District close to Barrie's home.

We thank Brian and Barrie for allowing us to view their collection of Heiron paintings and letting us photograph some of these priceless originals. We also thank John Holmes-Higgin for permission to reproduce the painting of the 'Flying Scotsman' featured on page 76.

Special thanks must go to Andrew McArthur who photographed the bulk of the paintings reproduced in this book.

Finally we thank George for expressing his 'art' form whether through the camera or painted canvas.

Ashley Hill bank, Bristol — no wonder it made a greater appeal to the young George Heiron than Sunday School! A February 1955 study of the northbound 'Devonian' on its journey from Kingswear to Bradford. The engines are Stanier 'Black Five' No 45262 and 'Jubilee' No 45682 *Trafalgar*, and there are freight trains on either side. The 'Devonian' took the former Great Western route out of the city to Filton and ran via the Westerleigh Junctions to reach the Midland route to Birmingham.

GH: Ashley Hill station, at the top of the picture, the bridge carrying the Avonmouth Docks line to the north, the two inner tracks below — all are gone with regret. Just two tracks remain nowadays on this busy exit from Bristol!

Making a Start

George Heiron was born in 1929. He was brought up in Bristol, not far from Ashley Hill on the north-east side of the city and fortunately near the railway. He recalls playing truant from Sunday School when he was five years old or so, in order to watch trains toiling up the steep climb taking them out of the city, up towards Filton and on to the Severn Tunnel.

Asked if this incident marked the start of his interest in railways, George pauses for a moment in his recollections. 'The first locomotive I remember clearly was No 6000 *King George V* which I saw at Temple Meads when my mother took me to the station to watch trains. My interest in railways just took off from there!'

Before long, that keenness for railways began another association. At the age of five or six he submitted a pen and ink drawing to the old *Bristol Evening World* newspaper and it was published. George comments: 'I think the subject of the drawing was a GWR "King". My father was disapproving, and commented, "You could do better than that!" '

His mother was the artistic influence in the family and indeed was art mistress at the West of England College of Art. George was growing up in the late 1930s, that anxious epoch preceding the outbreak of World War 2. The Heiron family was bombed out in one of the ferocious air-raids on the city early in 1941 and forced to leave Bristol. For the next decade or so the Heirons lived at Tolldown, near Dyrham, eight miles north of Bath.

George joined the staff of the Bristol Aeroplane Company on leaving school towards the end of the war. The factory at Filton was engaged principally in making Hercules engines for Bristol Beaufighter aircraft and his first post was in the blueprint office. By now he was taking photographs of trains. 'I wasn't really a photographer in the true sense of the word — only taking pictures with my Mum's box camera. I was also painting railways for interest.'

He wanted to take art seriously and soon left the blueprint office to study art at the West of England College of Art in Bristol. He was there for five years. Once qualified, he took up a job as an artist at the well-known city firm of E. S. & A. Robinson, Fishponds. His principal work there involved line drawings. It was either that or painting. George says that neither crayons nor chalks have ever appealed to him.

Next came National Service. In 1949 George was posted to Benghazi and joined the 26th Field Regiment, Royal Artillery. It was not long before he became the official regimental signwriter and was given his own workshop. 'I was more or less my own boss, except when I had to take part in occasional manoeuvres in the desert as a 10-ton truck driver. I was working on some signs one morning when I had the surprise of my life. General Montgomery marched briskly in with the RSM for a chat. He stayed talking about one thing and another, including his old battlegrounds in the vicinity. After about 15 minutes he departed with a cheerful remark, "Well, have a good holiday!" which of course it was.'

'I was later posted to Malta, another "holiday" and again as a signwriter. The last six months before demob took me to Egypt and the Canal Zone. There was a light railway near where we were based. I was soon taking photographs of British military workings and the trains of Egyptian State Railways. I remember clearly one photograph was of a War Department Stanier "8F" 2-8-0 fitted with a cowcatcher. It was fairly clean — not like the "8Fs" in service back home. One of the "8Fs" hit a camel and was derailed. That engine stayed on its side in the desert for some time.'

'After my stint of National Service had finished in 1951, I decided that I didn't want a job where I would be shut indoors. I became self-employed and undertook signwriting, as well as painting. It was a fairly hectic life! My commissions included painting rolls of honour in colleges. In particular, I worked at Clifton College and also at the University of Bristol.

It called for a steady hand, all that gold lettering. It also took a toll of my eyesight.'

'The signwriting included painting shopfronts and fascias. One job was for a shop at Pucklechurch and I had to paint a big polar bear which was the trademark for Eldorado, the long-defunct ice cream firm.'

'Then there were the inn-signs. I used Humbrol model paint which I varnished over. Some of the inn-signs had railway subjects. One was for the

Making a start — with Mum's Box Brownie. At the head of a stopping train to Swindon is brand-new 'County' 4-6-0 No 1018 *County of Leicester* which was photographed in 1946 from the platform slope at Bristol Temple Meads.

Great Western Hotel, Yeovil, and featured a "King" rushing out of Box Tunnel. An inn-sign for The Folly, Downend, had as its subject a miner in a flooded mine. You see — the folly of a miner working a flooded mine! Lots of the coal mines in this area suffered from flooding. Another inn-sign was for *The Bell*, Chipping Sodbury. I decided not to make use of a local theme. Instead, I set it in Mexico and painted a stone archway with a bell hanging below, with mountains in the background. People threw stones at the bell and eventually either the landlord or the brewery removed the sign!'

In the early 1950s fewer people were self-employed than today and it took considerable confidence and perseverance to build up a living based on signwriting and painting. George's self-reliance has stood him in good stead over the years. He has succeeded because he was good at his work and has always delivered his commissions on time.

**The early days of the 'Britannias' on the Western Region. Taking advantage of falling grades, the up 'Red Dragon'
rounds the curve near Hullavington behind 'Britannia' No 70029 *Shooting Star*.**
GH: **One of my earlier photographs, dating from 1952 and not long after I had completed National Service. It was a
frosty day and I crouched down to get my picture. Marvellous exhaust!**

Roaming the Rails with a Camera

Despite all the pressures of working for himself, George was out and about photographing trains during 1951/52. Living at Tolldown meant that the South Wales main line sweeping through north-west Wiltshire and south Gloucestershire was within easy cycling distance, as was the Bristol main line on its approaches to Bath. Some of the photographic locations had become well-known to George earlier than that. With Shirley we travelled out to some of his old stamping-grounds early in 2000. As the three of us looked north from an overbridge at Rangeworthy that takes a lane over the former Midland main line from Bristol to Birmingham, George commented: 'I discovered this section back in 1945.'

While he was always careful to seek out good vantage-points for photography, he was also attracted to particular locomotive types. 'I had been in the Army for a couple of years and during that time the British Railways Standard Pacifics had entered service. These were the "Britannias" — they hadn't been built when I went overseas on National Service. What lovely engines! Some of them had burnished rims to their wheels and the "Britannias" allocated to Cardiff Canton shed were kept particularly clean. During this period, and particularly in the snow, I photographed the "Britannias" a lot on the main line through Badminton.'

And thereby hangs a tale, for George was to establish Badminton station and its vicinity as one of the classic locations of steam age photographs. All that is in the past because the station was closed to passengers in 1968 and soon afterwards demolished. The history of this stretch of railway and of the station itself provides a fascinating backdrop to those evocative wintry or night-time studies.

The 33-mile South Wales & Bristol Direct Railway resulted from discontent among the industrialists of South Wales who complained of the Great Western Railway's monopoly of the route to London, which in those days took through trains on the exit from the Severn Tunnel past Bristol and through Bath. They proposed an entirely new London & South Wales Railway from Cardiff, crossing the Severn Estuary on a mighty bridge and then continuing past Malmesbury, Cricklade and Oxford on its way to the capital. But the South Wales promoters were persuaded to reach agreement with the GWR at the eleventh hour before the Bill for the new railway was to be deposited in Parliament. The basis of that agreement was that the GWR would itself construct a new length of main line from near Patchway, on Bristol's northern outskirts, to Wootton Bassett, five or so miles west of Swindon, where it would make a junction with Brunel's route between Paddington and Bristol.

Authorised in 1896, the new line was not opened to traffic until the summer of 1903. It features heavy engineering works which were essential in maintaining a ruling gradient of 1 in 300. There are high embankments, deep cuttings, four viaducts, a lengthy tunnel at Chipping Sodbury which took the railway under a spur of the Cotswolds for a distance of 2½ miles, and the much shorter Alderton Tunnel to its east.

For most of its earlier years the line seldom attracted railway photographers, except at its western end where the Bristol-based G. H. Soole (whose negatives are now in the National Railway Museum's photographic archives) was active in the late 1930s. The main line's grandeur with its fine range of engineering structures provided a foil for the South Wales expresses as they travelled at speed along the down grades, and on their exit from South Wales toiled upgrade to the line's summit just to the east of Badminton. George Heiron made the line the setting for some of his most arresting and dramatic photography.

There is more to say about Badminton station itself. Back in 1897, the Dowager Duchess of Beaufort had cut the first sod for the construction of the line which passed through the family's lands. A station was duly built at Badminton and, unsurprisingly perhaps, the Beaufort coat of arms featured on a plaque that formed the stonework of one of the platform buildings. From the start of services over the line, privileged first-class passengers could ask for fast trains to make a special stop at Badminton, the privilege applying to the family and guests of the Duke of Beaufort travelling to and from Badminton House. Later, a conditional stop at Badminton was inserted in the schedules of several London-South Wales expresses, such as the 3.55pm from Paddington. In

Making the Badminton stop — a westbound express pauses on a summer evening. The engine just clear of the overbridge is 'Britannia' No 70026 *Polar Star*.

postwar days, the by now mandatory Badminton stop featured not only in the schedule of the 3.55pm down, which from 1956 was named the 'Capital United Express', but also the 5.55pm ex-Paddington which from 1950 had carried the stirring title of the 'Red Dragon'. Up South Wales expresses called at Badminton — the up morning Fishguard boat train, and an evening express on weekdays and Sundays alike. George's shot from ground-level of a 'Britannia' at the head of one of these trains making the Badminton stop on a frosty January evening particularly lingers in the memory.

The station at Badminton followed the neat and business-like architectural style adopted by the GWR for its early 20th century stations. It was smartly kept and George recalls the attractive flower-beds and hanging baskets that were the pride of the station staff. Badminton station was laid out with two platform roads for those passenger trains stopping there, or freight trains being 'put inside' — to use railway parlance — to allow a faster train to precede them. The ensemble was completed by a canopied passengers' footbridge at the western end of the station, on the Bristol side of which there was a bridge with a girder span that carried the road to Badminton village (and Badminton House) over the main line. At this end of the station the line ran through a shallow cutting.

Picture the scene, then, as either one of the two down South Wales expresses made its Badminton stop at 5.44pm or 7.58pm respectively on a winter's evening. George explains his technique: 'I began night photography at Badminton in 1953. I always gave myself plenty of time. I knew where the train usually stopped — with the engine just clear on the west side of the overbridge. There was a convenient bank on which to stand and from where I had a marvellous view. I noticed how the lights of the carriages interiors shone out — and in the right conditions would be reflected on the snow.'

'One night I stood there in the snow for nearly an hour — the train was late as a result of frozen points somewhere on the way from Paddington. I was standing in snow up to my knees. Before long, the stationmaster, escorted by a porter carrying a hand-lamp, trudged through the snow off the end of Badminton station platform and approached me: "What are you doing?" said the stationmaster. 'Freezing!', I replied. "You must want your head reading!" was his retort. When one of my night shots taken at Badminton was published in *Trains Illustrated*, his attitude changed,' recalls George. 'From then on I was provided with tea in the station master's house.'

And that of course was the secret — the credit 'G. F. Heiron' was increasingly appearing below photographs reproduced in *Trains Illustrated*, the monthly railway journal published by Ian Allan Ltd and edited by the late Geoffrey Freeman Allen. *Trains Illustrated* outshone its contemporaries on account of its high-quality production and a judicious blend of incisive comment on current developments on Britain's railways, well-written historical articles and clever use of the best of current railway photography.

From 1953 George Heiron's pictures were increasingly a feature of *Trains Illustrated*. The January 1953 issue had featured George's study of Western Region gas turbine locomotive No 18100 pulling away from Bath at the head of a Bristol express. In those days the very few main line diesel and two gas turbine locomotives were newsworthy. The Western Region gas turbines in particular were far from regular performers and spent much of their time undergoing attention in the workshops or on shed.

The style of the *Trains Illustrated* of the time derived from the half-tone reproductions printed from typical letterpress blocks whose screen is coarse by modern standards of printing, A. F. Wolstenholme's lino-cuts, and a characteristic fifties typography. It made for a beguiling mixture, and today the atmosphere of the steam-operated British Railways of the period comes across more strongly from these modest magazines than from a score of videos employing carefully edited contemporary ciné film.

The photographers that had been most often represented in the pages of *Trains Illustrated* had been Eric Treacy, E. D. Bruton and E. R. Wethersett, all of whom were older than George. His work, however, had caught Geoffrey Freeman Allen's eye for his photographs were increasingly being featured in the magazine. Over the years, Freeman — as he was most usually known to the world of railway publishing — regularly corresponded with George, to keep him appraised of forthcoming features appearing in the magazine and indeed other Ian Allan publications.

Take the run of *Trains Illustrated* for the year 1954. The January issue had a full-page reproduction of George's October 1953 study of an LMS Standard '2P' 4-4-0 piloting a 'West Country' Pacific out of Bath with the 'Pines Express' on the last stage of its 7¼hr southbound journey from Manchester to Bournemouth. The landscape format, half-tone illustration was opposite 'Talking of Trains' — the magazine's editorial news and views page. With the February 1954 issue, one of George's prints had been selected for the cover picture, an accolade keenly sought by photographers. Its subject was one of his favourites — 'Britannia' Pacific No 70028

The Metrovick gas turbine locomotive No 18100 spent a limited time working on the Western Region. It is seen departing from Bath Spa station with the down 'Merchant Venturer' on 2 July 1952.

**The 12noon Bristol Temple Meads-Paddington express rounds the wide curve below Shockerwick and begins the climb
to Box Tunnel. The engine is 'Castle' 4-6-0 No 5095 *Barbury Castle* and the date, 10 August 1953. This photograph was
first reproduced in the February 1954 *Trains Illustrated*.**

Royal Star on the final stage of the climb out of Severn Tunnel, passing Chipping Sodbury in October 1953 at the head of the up 'Red Dragon' express. Facing 'Talking of Trains' in that issue was George's August 1953 picture of a 'Castle' sweeping round the curve of the approach to Box Tunnel with a Bristol-Paddington express. Another half-tone was inset into the sky of this picture which ruined much of its impact.

This was his other favourite main line in the vicinity of his home — Brunel's Bristol-Paddington trunk route on its approaches to and through the city of Bath, then up from Bathampton to Box Tunnel. Any of the locations was an easy bike ride from home. The location of the photograph reproduced in the February 1954 issue was Shockerwick — on the easier grades leading to the climb at 1 in 100 through Box Tunnel. 'The stretch

'Picture Parade' choice for the May 1954 issue of *Trains Illustrated*: with a 2-6-2T assisting at the rear of its train for the climb to Sapperton, an ex-GWR '2884' 2-8-0 crosses Frampton Viaduct with a Gloucester-Swindon freight, January 1954.

of railway from Chippenham and through Box station — a mile south of the tunnel — was certainly one of my favourites. From the now closed and demolished station at Box there was a pathway beside the line which was ideal for taking pictures. You could walk over Box Middle Hill and look down over the railway and up to Box Tunnel itself. You can't get near there now for trees and bushes that

have grown up over the past 40 years. Just up the line at Shockerwick was a footbridge that took a cross-country path over the railway line.'

One feature of the *Trains Illustrated* of the period was its regular photographic feature, 'Picture Parade', which served as a showcase for some of the most arresting images of trains of the period. In the May 1954 issue another of George's favoured

locations was the setting of a beautifully lit wintry shot of a Great Western 2-8-0 at grips with the climb out of the Golden Valley and up to Sapperton Tunnel, assistance being provided at the rear end of the train by a 2-6-2T.

There's a story behind one of George's next pictures to appear in *Trains Illustrated*. On 25 April 1954, Ian Allan organised a rail tour that travelled from Waterloo to Bournemouth, then took the Somerset & Dorset Joint line to Bath Green Park station. After time for sightseeing in the city, participants on the rail tour returned home via Templecombe, where the train joined the Southern Region's West of England main line to steam through Salisbury and on through Basingstoke to regain Waterloo. The particular 'selling-point' perhaps was the first-ever provision of 'Schools' class 4-4-0 No 30932 *Blundells* to work from Waterloo to Bath (piloted by a locally-based engine from Bournemouth), and again from Templecombe to Waterloo. From Bath to Templecombe a brace of LMS Standard '2P' 4-4-0s were used, to allow the 'Schools' to run light engine ahead of the train from Bath and to be turned at its leisure at Templecombe before the arrival of the special.

George's picture of the pair of '2Ps' at the head of the train on its return run as it emerged from Bath's Devonshire Tunnel was duly published in the June 1954 *Trains Illustrated*. 'I remember that day well. Ivo Peters (a well-known railway photographer of the 1950s and 1960s) was there with his Bentley car. I had cycled there and I was just in my shorts. He wouldn't speak to me as I waited to get my shot. We both photographed the special train with the "2Ps" — and it was mine that was published in *Trains Illustrated*. Ivo Peters had a tripod — what did he want with a tripod in daytime, anyway?'

'I didn't meet that many railway photographers, but I must say that the majority of them were friendly. Most of them have passed on now. I had been going to meet Eric Treacy just before he collapsed and died in 1978 at Appleby station where he had gone to photograph a special steam working over the Settle & Carlisle line.'

George used to go photographing trains with friends. 'One chap lived in Chippenham. We took photographs of the same trains, but he was aiming for a purely mechanical effect. He didn't want to include the scenery, no smoke if at all possible, just the engine coming towards you.'

Individual photographs submitted by George appeared in other 1954 issues of *TI* and a particularly handsome pair were chosen by Freeman for the centrespread of the September issue which featured four prints presented under one of Freeman's typically wry titles — 'Trains in the sunshine ... nostalgic memories for a dismal summer'. George's studies came from days spent alongside the Standish Junction-Swindon main line. One is a May '54 rear three-quarters picture of a Cheltenham-Paddington express on the steepest part of the climb to Sapperton Tunnel, illustrating how the railway winds its way through the valley. George remarks of the impact made by this

photograph: 'In the 1950s approaching Sapperton you could see the track weaving along the valley. This locality is like a forest now.'

The second of the 'Trains in the Sunshine' pictures was most certainly in the sunshine but had been taken on a typical early April day of light and shadows. Its subject was a train of anthracite coal from South Wales trudging up a straight length of the same main line behind an ex-War Department 2-8-0, the plume of smoke from the train engine echoed by another from the Brimscombe banking engine that was lending a hand at the rear of the train.

One other George Heiron picture used in the 1954 issues of *Trains Illustrated* deserves particular mention. It was a summery picture of a 'Castle' making the approach to Bathampton with a Paddington-Bristol-Plymouth express. The engine and train are nicely lit by the westering sun. Behind

the train is a dramatic sky with a bank of cumulonimbus clouds. From the time of the train mentioned, the exposure must have been made at about 6.30pm.

'I was always on the look-out for a sky — a fine day for artists and photographers. These evening shots made for a pleasant cycle ride out and back from home. I was always interested in landscape and cloudscape — it was a matter of fitting the railway into it.'

From his home at Tolldown, George could take his pick of three main lines, the third being the former Midland Railway main line from Bristol past Westerleigh Junction, Yate and Wickwar. Six or so miles particularly appealed to George and in the 4½ miles between Wickwar and Yate stations came Wickwar Tunnel and Rangeworthy — the latter being the location of a now vanished signalbox near the summit of a rising section of line.

In the foreground, one of George's photographer friends, Raymond Thomas of Chippenham, concentrates on the essentials as 'Castle' 4-6-0 No 7015 *Carn Brea Castle* coasts out of Sapperton Tunnel and begins the descent into the Golden Valley with a lightweight express for Gloucester and Cheltenham, March 1956. An ex-Great Northern Railway corridor brake composite is next the engine.

'From my house to Rangeworthy took just 15 minutes by bike. I went out quickly in the evening when the position of the sun and the lighting conditions were just right. Along this stretch, with the railway curving gently in a north-easterly direction, there was wonderful side lighting from the setting sun on a June evening.'

George knew the farmers in the vicinity of Rangeworthy, one of whom was a railway enthusiast. Rich and well-tended farmland seen in the light of the setting sun features in so many of his finest studies, usually of 'Jubilee' 4-6-0s on the last stretch of a lengthy through working from the north, or else getting into their stride with the 7.20pm Bristol Temple Meads-Newcastle Travelling Post Office train.

Comments George: 'Wickwar was one of my favourite locations — nice countryside, nice scenery. Fortunately, the locality is still unspoilt today.' As we found on our recent excursion by car, that doesn't mean that it remains ideal for railway photography. Hedges have grown up along the lineside and sizeable trees have taken hold in the cutting leading to Wickwar Tunnel.

'In steam days,' George recalls, 'I was out here all the time. Had a pocketful of films. There was one train behind the other. You couldn't see the southern portal of Wickwar Tunnel — it was always full of smoke from passing trains.'

'When it came to the northbound "Devonian" express from Paignton to Bradford that was booked to leave Bristol Temple Meads at 12.30pm, half an hour later the lighting conditions were ideal at the north portal of Wickwar Tunnel.' Choosing a suitable angle from which to take the photograph was not a problem on the railway of the 1950s. George continues: 'You could walk up the track from the level crossing in Wickwar village — it led to the stationmaster's house.'

That track is no longer there, but in any case — for totally understandable reasons, given the incidence of trespass and vandalism on today's railways — to attempt to do the same today would result in the driver of a passing train using his 'ship to shore' radio to advise the British Transport Police of a trespasser. Before long a patrol car would be on the scene.

The gradual encroachment of trees and bushes at

The northern portal of Wickwar Tunnel: the 'Devonian' express is heading north to the Midlands, and eventually Leeds and Bradford. Its engine is Bristol-based 'Jubilee' 4-6-0 No 45662 *Kempenfelt*.

That location near St Anne's Park station, between Keynsham and Bristol. The tunnel is known as St Anne's Wood. Heading the down 'Merchant Venturer' express from Paddington to Bristol Temple Meads and Weston-super-Mare is double chimney 'Castle' 4-6-0 No 7019 *Fowey Castle*.
GH: This provided the reference for a painting commissioned by *Model Railway News* — I added three young ladies in the foreground!

Salisbury in steam days. Working the up 'Atlantic Coast Express' is recently rebuilt 'Merchant Navy' Pacific No 35023
Holland-Afrika Line. **Nicely judged action with the enginemen and the train-spotters. This photograph was published as**
a double-spread, in typical fashion, by the US railfan journal, *Trains.*

the lineside has also ruled out locations such as St Anne's Park which lies between Keynsham and the outskirts of Bristol. Just to the east of the now closed station at St Anne's Park is an ornate tunnel portal. Parallel to the track, and providing an unrivalled location for taking a photograph of a train emerging from the tunnel, was a footpath guarded by GWR spear-type fencing on either side. 'You can't get there now', remarks George. 'The footpath is no

longer there.' In steam days George would cycle to a convenient point for a favoured stretch of main line. 'I'd put the bike in a hedge, set off on foot exploring — spend all day photographing!'

Shirley Tanner, the future Mrs Heiron, cycled out with George on these expeditions. 'He took me out and I tried to help. I wanted to know what made engines *go*!'

While George is associated with a number of

locations in the area bounded by Chippenham, Charfield, Patchway and Bristol, he also photographed elsewhere — either when on holiday or during a day's outing by bike. Sometimes he took his bike by train to extend his range.

'There was so much steam near where I lived that I didn't need to go further afield', he comments. When he did, the sort of outings he undertook say much about the lifestyle of 40-50 years ago, not least that the relatively low levels of road traffic of the time made long-distance cycle rides both practicable and pleasant. These days there is a greater risk of danger, not to mention continual exposure to vehicle exhaust fumes.

'I used to go roaming about like a cowboy. I'd take sandwiches and a jam roll and think nothing of cycling to Salisbury — 50 miles cycling there, 50 miles back. I spent all day running up and down the line. I was fit in those days all right!'

Salisbury was a lively railway centre in steam days, with the Bulleid Pacific-hauled Waterloo-West of England expresses, cross-country expresses to and from the South Coast via Westbury and Southampton, and heavy freight traffic moving over the former GWR line from Westbury and Warminster. Says George: 'I used to walk alongside the SR Exeter line beyond Wilton South and out along the chalk downs.' I asked if he had gone to the east of Salisbury station, to Tunnel Junction, where the lines to Worting Junction and Romsey parted. 'I never went there — never knew about it.'

BRISTOL ALBUM
Photographed by
GEORGE HEIRON

Above: "Castle" Class 4-6-0 No. 5085 *Evesham Abbey* eases the 5.15 p.m. from Weston-Super-Mare past Bath Road shed and into Temple Meads station.
Below: A ''Hall'' 4-6-0 on a West-to-North express and a Class "2" 2-6-2T on a Bath (Green Park) local set off together from Temple Meads.

NEXT TWO PAGES
Top left: A "6959" Class 4-6-0 sets out from Temple Meads for Shrewsbury with the 12.0 noon Penzance-Crewe.
Bottom left: No. 6814 *Enborne Grange* on an incoming train from Weston-Super-Mare greets a sister "Grange" 4-6-0 leaving Temple Meads on the 5.30 a.m. Paddington-Plymouth.
Top right: As 2-6-2T No. 5553 shunts stock on the left, the Saturday 8.10 a.m. Newport-Paignton curves into Temple Meads double-headed by No. 6838 *Goodmoor Grange* and a "6959" Class 4-6-0. On the extreme left of the picture the turrets of Temple Meads facade are showing; to the right of them is the spire of St. Mary Redcliffe's church.
Bottom right: An earlier shot of the 8.10 a.m. Newport-Paignton as it approached the photographer's vantage point.

The first page of the 'Bristol Album' photo-feature from the December 1957 *Trains Illustrated*.

George at Edinburgh Waverley, 1955 — but not one of the pictures selected for the feature appearing in the December 1956 *Trains Illustrated*. Peppercorn 'A1' Pacific No 60159 *Bonnie Dundee* departs from the station with an express for Aberdeen.

In any case, there was plenty to see at Salisbury station, with the Pacifics on the West of England trains being watered and the coal in their tenders being pulled forward during the station stop. 'I remember the "Merchant Navy" class engines slipping violently when they restarted their trains from the station. There was a café outside the station, underneath the arches carrying the railway over Fisherton Street. I was in there with a friend one day and the vibration from a "Merchant Navy" brought the ceiling down.'

There were longer cycle rides. One was to an aunt who lived in Watford, others were 4hr journeys to Sutton, Surrey, or Romford when he went through London on his bike — and out the other side. 'On

the occasion I went to Romford, I got to central London in the rush-hour and was walled-in by buses — couldn't get out.' The return from Watford saw him set off for home at 9pm, cycling through the night. Nearing home, he was cycling along the Old London Road, a section of highway once used by stage-coaches. It was 3am. A curious vehicle was approaching him — it seemed to be a cross between a stage-coach and an old-style London taxicab. 'The apparition made no sound — it just floated past. I went cold,' says George.

Another railway trip took George to Scotland in 1955 when he stayed with a friend at New Cumnock, Ayrshire. That explains how a 'G. F. Heiron' credit appears below a picture of a rebuilt 'Royal Scot'

A summer Saturday express for Birmingham New Street departs from Platform 7 at Bristol Temple Meads behind
BR Standard '5' 4-6-0 No 73038.
GH: **This was one of the photographs taken from the roof of the paint factory.**

Action featuring the up 'Bristolian' of the late 1950s as it heads past Stoke Gifford freight yards behind an immaculate 'Castle'. The obvious urgency of the express contrasts with rows of stationary wagons in the sidings. The usual seven-coach load of the 'Bristolian' has been increased by the addition of the Western Region's track-recording coach at the rear. The up 'Bristolian' was routed via Filton Junction and Badminton but the down train ran via Bath.

passing near Carronbridge with the Glasgow-bound 'Thames-Clyde Express'. In the December 1956 *Trains Illustrated*, Freeman Allen pushed out the boat with a seven-page photo-feature entitled, 'Festival of Steam'. Its typically tongue-in-cheek intro reads: 'Once a year, Edinburgh puts on its great Festival of the Arts. All the year round the Scottish capital is the busy meeting-place of East and West Coast steam, from Pacifics to graceful pre-1923 types.'

The photographs chosen for 'Festival of Steam' came from the cameras of Eric Treacy and George Heiron, with a solitary contribution from Bill Anderson. George was particularly intrigued by Princes Street Gardens, which provided him with a grandstand view of trains departing from the west end of Edinburgh Waverley station. One picture cleverly includes bystanders who seemingly share George's enthusiasm at the simultaneous departure at 4pm of two LNER-design Pacifics, one at the head of an express to Glasgow Queen Street, the other on the Perth train. The trains headed out on parallel tracks through Princes Street Gardens.

Trains Illustrated was keen on photo-portraits of cities and their railways. George was at home in his native Bristol, always aware of suitable buildings that might provide him with unusual vantage-points of trains arriving at or departing from Temple Meads station.

'I would walk up and down dirty old back streets. I knew at one point I could climb up a parapet behind one of the signalboxes at the approaches to Temple Meads. Bedminster Park was a fine place from which to take pictures, also there was a good vantage-point at Totterdown, on high land on the west side of the station. I knew where I could get permission to enter the back garden of a house where I could obtain a panoramic view of the whole station. Another useful location for taking photographs of trains approaching Temple Meads was the roof of the Rainbow paint factory, and I had no difficulty in getting permission for access.'

This careful detective work and long-term reconnaissance paid off for he had amassed a unique collection of photographs of Bristol's railways. The material was put to good use by *Trains Illustrated* for 'Bristol Album', a seven-page feature in the December 1957 issue. The credit was straight to the point, 'photographed by George Heiron', it read.

There were trains coming into and out of Temple Meads station, and a couple of fine studies of the city's premier train, the 'Bristolian', the steam-worked express of the mid-1950s which was booked in just 1¾hr for its non-stop journey from and to Paddington. One shot in 'Bristol Album' was of the up train storming up Ashley Hill bank just as another 'Castle' fortuitously comes into the picture from the left. The other is a classic study of No 7014 *Caerhays Castle* passing Dr Day's Bridge Junction signalbox on the first stage of its trip to Paddington. Two years later, the 'Bristolian' was handed over to diesel traction and it wasn't long before a Heiron picture of a 'Warship' diesel-hydraulic passing Dr Day's Bridge Junction signalbox had appeared in an Ian Allan publication.

Ten miles from Bristol Temple Meads were the Westerleigh Junctions — North, East and West — where the former GWR Paddington-South Wales main line crosses the Midland's Birmingham-Bristol route. The layout was rationalised and resignalled 30 or more years ago. In their old form the Westerleigh Junctions and the line past Stoke Gifford marshalling yard provided George with a happy stamping-ground: 'This section of line was very busy — still is — and I was always interested to see the banana trains that had originated at Avonmouth.' A couple of particularly effective shots

from Stoke Gifford included trains speeding past the sorting sidings — a clever juxtaposition of the spectacle of a fast-moving express with serried rows of static freight vehicles.

Westerleigh provided the location for a July evening photograph that was sheer luck — a 'Britannia' speeding west with the 'Red Dragon' was caught on film just about to pass a 2-8-0 plodding uphill with freight from South Wales.

South Wales (and Monmouthshire) tended to be neglected by railway photographers into relatively recent years when the decline of industrial steam acted as a catalyst. The area certainly provided George with scope for interesting images, particularly train movements in and around Cardiff General and Newport stations. He admits, however, that he never ventured further west.

The action was not restricted to the trackside for he has always been fascinated by railway booking halls and restaurants at busy times. So it was that George was able to offer a wonderful range of prints for Freeman Allen to illustrate a two-part article that

appeared early in 1959 for one of the classic *Trains Illustrated* series, 'Resorts for Railfans'.

The 'resort' was Cardiff. The text provided by William Jones and John Hodge, joint contributors of a comprehensive survey of the history and current operations of railways serving the city, was complemented by George Heiron's views not just of the trains but also the façade and interior of Cardiff General station, some atmospheric shots of engines on Cardiff Canton shed, and of recently dieselised local services. The Canton loco shed pictures include some fine studies of steam power. What is not obvious is that George was escorted by Shirley round the cinder-strewn shed yard, no doubt with its fair share of oily puddles and grease-encrusted sleepers. 'I remember it well,' she recalls. 'I was wearing a green dress and high-heeled shoes!'

George and Shirley were married in 1959. Before steam working had finished on the West Highland they took their tandem bike with them on the Fort William sleeping car train from London King's Cross. On that 1961 trip, in a cleverly planned

The sort of photograph that summed-up South Wales in the steam age — extensive wagonload traffic and plenty of train movements. '43xx' 2-6-0 No 6323 'rumbles towards Cardiff', reads George's caption of the time, 'past Newton West Goods box with a freight train'. One of the pictures used to illustrate that 'Resorts for Railfans' two-part article in *Trains Illustrated*.

Shirley Heiron was nobly escorting George around the grime of Cardiff Canton shed yard when he obtained this study of BR Standard '9F' 2-10-0 No 92222 and an ex-War Department Austerity 2-8-0, whose own tender and that of the engine in front of it contain some decent lumps of coal.

Headed by a BR Standard 4-6-0 and an ex-LMS '5' 4-6-0, the afternoon restaurant car express to Fort William awaits the 'right-away' from Glasgow Queen Street in March 1961. George and Shirley — and their tandem — were bound for the Highlands.
GH: **All done on Kodak Super XX film, with my standard exposure of f11 and a shutter speed of ½₅₀ second.**

photograph taken at Glasgow Queen Street High Level station, George made good use of the available light in the partially subterranean terminus, notable in steam days for being almost continually enveloped in a pall of smoke. George and Shirley cycled from Fort William to Mallaig. 'We saw just one car in all those miles and a post-lady on her bike,' says George. 'We returned by train to Fort William which was our base. We used the tandem to get to the Monessie Gorge and on to Rannoch Moor.' Shirley smiles. 'I was at the back of the tandem and I used to sing as we cycled.'

George and Shirley's son, Richard, has inherited the photographic skill. For some years he was a salesman in the photographic and video department of the John Lewis Partnership's departmental store in Broadmead, Bristol. He was also official photographer at the Partnership's business meetings and dinners, and numerous yacht outings off the South Coast. Now he is manager of a camera shop.

To return, however, to the early 1960s when steam was giving way to diesel and electric traction throughout British Railways. It's as good a time as any to return to when George was out and about in the Indian Summer of steam, adopting fresh approaches to railway photography that ensured his name would be to the forefront in railway publications. To start with the basics, which cameras and accessories was he using?

'I had begun with my Mother's old Brownie Box camera. Then came a Voigtlander 2¼in, three Zeiss models including a 2¼ and a 3¼in, and more recently a Mamiya Press camera with a roll film adaptor. I believed in keeping accessories to a minimum. I had no more than two filters, a yellow one for general use in sunshine and an orange one for landscape and dramatic sky effects. I have never used a light meter!'

'My preferred film was Kodak Super XX film, 120 size. I did all the processing and developing and frequently stayed up until 2am enlarging and printing. In my opinion, the old grades of paper such as Kodak Bromide were best — you could get the half-shades. With the resin-coated papers that were introduced generally in the 1970s you lost the middle tones in a picture.'

Certainly, the combination of the old photographic papers and the effect of letterpress printing has conditioned the way that we perceive steam in action at a time when its supremacy had yet to be challenged. Sometimes you wish that many of the steam photographers of old had employed a little more imagination. But, then, in selecting photographs for reproduction the *Railway Magazine* editorial staff of the 1930s and 1940s marked up the prints for cropping photographs in accordance with

their conventions of what 'looked right' in terms of half-tone reproductions. Their conservatism stifled innovation and it needed someone of the stature of Eric Treacy to defy the editorial staff to do their worst. It is all the more disappointing when you see what some US and French railway photographers had to offer back in the 1930s and the way their material was used.

George took a less conventional approach to his photography. He asked if I had seen copies of the US railfan magazine *Trains* dating from the early 1950s, in the days when it was edited by the legendary, David T. Morgan. Photographs appearing in *Trains* had provided George with useful inspiration. He liked the way that American photographers tended to include trackmen or enginemen in their shots of trains and he copied some of their approach. It was not, however, a one-way process, as George had the honour of having one of his photographs of a 'Castle' at speed on a Bristol express published in the June 1954 issue of *Trains*. Other pictures of his have also appeared in this journal.

Inevitably, the conversation turned to O. Winston Link and to George's success with night photography which he had first tried at Badminton station in 1953, the subject of the first essay being a 'Castle'. It is worth noting that Link's five-year 'project' — as he called it — involving the night photography of steam trains began only in January 1955. George Heiron was a pioneer with his first experiments in 1953, at a time when as Link mentions in his book *Night Trick by O. Winston Link* (The Photographer's Gallery/National Railway Museum, 1983) he had just been inspired to record steam at night. To quote O. Winston Link, 'I had to make a move. Steam was on the way out!'

So how did George go about night photography? 'I used a big open flash-gun with a long reflector — much more effective than synchronised flash. The bulbs were bigger than a domestic light-bulb and it was a case of one bulb, one flash. Mind you, in the

Among the first of many of George's night shots — 'Castle' 4-6-0 No 7032 *Denbigh Castle* waits at Badminton station with a Paddington-South Wales express in 1953. The double gables in the background are part of the signalmen's cottages. The stationmaster's house was considerably grander!

King's Cross at night. A pair of 'A4' Pacifics, No 60034 *Lord Faringdon* (nearest) and the immortal 60022 *Mallard* have arrived with expresses from the North. The vitrolite advertisements appearing above the arch were a long-lived feature of the terminus and lasted into recent years.

confines of a station they would light up a whole area — and that wouldn't be allowed today! One thing to watch was the glow from the open fire-door on an engine. Usually, I mounted the camera on a tripod and, having opened the lens, left it open for as long as possible, sometimes as much as eight minutes. I then walked to a spot side-on to the engine. Not all the night photographs that I took at Temple Meads made use of a tripod. Shirley would help me by flashing the gun.'

I looked at a night photograph of King's Cross featuring two 'A4s'. 'No flash', said George, 'that was a time-exposure, and of what I can remember from that occasion it was 10 seconds.'

I came across George's pleasantly expressed comments on the possibilities for night photography in the Introduction to his book *Trains to the West* (Ian Allan Ltd, 1978): 'Night scenes, I think, are particularly effective, especially in wet conditions, when trackwork, platforms and coach roofs glisten under station lights. An otherwise ordinary station scene can be transformed into a sparkling, magic world in a fine, steady drizzle — on celluloid if not literally!'

As another railway photographer once commented — it was the late-lamented Derek Cross — 'the most frustrating of all arts (is) photographing a moving train'. I asked about one of George

Heiron's most powerful photographs, a panned shot of a 'Britannia' running at speed which later formed the subject of one of his paintings. The engine was No 70027 *Rising Star* and it was photographed at Westerleigh in June 1956. For the record, that photograph made its first appearance in print in the November 1956 *Trains Illustrated*; since the question is bound to be asked, it was reproduced on page 568 of that issue!

Says George, 'I had experimented with panned shots — they were difficult to get right. You had to move the camera at the same speed as the train. The timing had to be exact — as you clicked the shutter the camera had to be kept moving in line with the train.'

Yet all is not what it seems. I looked with George at an attractive shot of a 'Castle' steaming west from Thingley Junction, near Chippenham, along a high embankment. 'I didn't pan it. That was taken on my old Zeiss, the shutter speed was ½50th of a second and the exposure was f16 using Kodak XX fast film. I remember that occasion clearly. There was no sound of road traffic — not as there would be at this same location today — there was just the magnificent sound of a steam express travelling at speed along the embankment.... '

This was the world of the 1950s when George enjoyed roaming the rails. In rural areas the railway passed through lonely miles of open country where the sounds of trains were challenged only by birdsong and the 'noises off' of farm animals and machinery. That world was changing in line with the rundown of steam traction on the railways. Increasingly, the roar of motor traffic was becoming the predominant sound-track in the countryside. What had inspired George was the way in which a railway signal cleared to green then, after a few minutes, a faint clatter rapidly grew to a crescendo

of sound as a train passed by on its journey. Then relative silence returned to the countryside. Now the sounds of trains were being swamped by those from road vehicles.

When it came to composing his photographs, George felt that where a diesel locomotive was the subject it needed strengthening in view of its weak aesthetic impact at track level. In one of his books of the 1970s he wrote: 'Its large, flat sides and ends, which resemble a motor lorry cab rather than a railway locomotive, cannot compare with the steam engine bristling with detail and "alive" with smoke and steam. Even a non-railway enthusiast could not resist the urge to whip out his camera at the sight and sound of a steam-hauled express.'

George feels that it is a real challenge to get the most from photographing diesel-hauled trains, calling for careful selection of background scenery, be it countryside, townscape or 'railwayscape'. His view is that diesels and electric locomotives are not themselves photogenic and their appeal is lessened further by the authorities' lack of imagination in choosing the livery schemes. In any case, any hope

of appeal is undermined because the locomotives are frequently either work-stained and, in the case of many of those allocated to the Western Region 30 and more years ago, their paint surfaces had been worn away by fuel spillage and the action of mechanical washing-plants.

That said, many of the most powerful images on film of the WR diesel-hydraulics and the Region's short-lived Blue Pullman diesel sets are the work of George Heiron. Badminton station continued to offer possibilities for night-time photography as 'Western' or Hymek diesel-hydraulics paused there with South Wales expresses but this traditional (perhaps one should say feudal) stop in Beaufort Country was doomed to early extinction with the closure of the station. With lights blazing from cabs and headcode indicator boxes, complemented by a breath of steam from the train heating hose, a main line diesel at Badminton still made for an arresting image.

George had continued to submit photographs to *Modern Railways* (as *Trains Illustrated* had been retitled from the January 1962 issue) as well as paintings for the publisher's other magazine titles

As an alternative to that famous panned shot of 1956, of a 'Britannia' Pacific hurrying down the inviting grades from Badminton station through Westerleigh, here is another, of sister engine No 70025 *Western Star* at speed with a South Wales express near Hullavington.

and books. He was also working with other notables in railway publishing, such as the late Patrick Whitehouse, and with *Model Railway News* and David St John Thomas. The impetus to getting together a portfolio of modern traction material came when he was commissioned in the late 1970s by Ian Allan Ltd to produce a photographic album that would intersperse some of his steam pictures of the 1950s and 1960s with those of current Western Region diesel traction.

Naturally, the cover of the resulting book — *Trains to the West* — featured one of George's paintings — of a 'Britannia' at Badminton — but the chosen black and white prints between its covers evenhandedly represented steam and diesel traction. By the time of the publication of *Trains to the West*, High Speed Trains had taken over almost all Paddington-Bristol and South Wales expresses from the diesel-hauled workings. While acknowledging the superior timetable offered to rail travellers, George admitted at the time that 'the hourly procession of regimented InterCity 125s' made it difficult for the photographer to be ambitious. Nonetheless, clear December sunshine and a sprinkling of snow by the lineside offered possibilities for interesting compositions.

Some of the impact of modern trains on well-loved railway routes was further explored in George's later photographic album, *Roaming the Western Rails* (Ian Allan Ltd, 1980). This saw him off on something like the expeditions of old, into Devon and Cornwall. He took his bike on the train to Plymouth, then cycled around Cornwall to get his pictures.

Railway observers of the late 1970s pointed to the fact that the replacement of steam by diesel and electric traction had been nothing like so major a revolution as other — and sometimes overlooked — changes to the railway infrastructure and services. Part of the impact of steam age photography relied on the composition incorporating semaphore signals, platelayers' huts and the lengthmen themselves. Mechanisation on the railway had 'taken out' signals and signalboxes. On-track machinery had taken over from labour-intensive maintenance. Lineside cabling laid in troughs displaced traditional 'line and pole' routes — the telegraph wires that had paralleled the track in the old days.

Something had been lost from the railway scene generally. Where once there had been bullhead rail in chairs laid on wooden sleepers, in turn riding on carefully manicured ballast, now main lines were being systemically modernised by the use of deep ballasting and track made up from continuously welded flat-bottom rail and heavy concrete sleepers.

With the demise of the lengthmen, no one was on hand to cut back cutting sides and to remove saplings before they could take hold. Although the environment of the modern railway was becoming more austere and rationalised, its overall impact was also deteriorating as vegetation took hold at the lineside, to change some locations out of all recognition.

Some of these issues provided subjects of discussion one April afternoon as I set out in the car with George and Shirley from their home in Coalpit Heath to revisit a couple of once-favoured photographic locations. This area to the north-east of Bristol has been gradually developed in recent years, not least as a result of the growth of Yate. 'Some locations were in the wilds in the 1950s and 60s,' comments George. 'Now the housing estates are encroaching.' On the South Wales main line, Wapley Common, near Chipping Sodbury, was the location of sidings and a wartime GWR signalbox and appears in several evening shots of the route's expresses. Hereabouts, the railway has been virtually submerged by housing development.

But we were bound for Rangeworthy and the Midland main line to Birmingham. Since the route rationalisation and resignalling of the 1960s, trains leave the old main line at Westerleigh Junction to take the former GWR South Wales line past Bristol Parkway station (built partly on the site of the old Stoke Gifford freight yards), then to travel via Filton and Stapleton Road into the centre of Bristol.

Not that this truncation has affected the scene at Rangeworthy, more precisely at Milepost 116¾ (as measured from the old Midland Railway headquarters at Derby). The fields of George's farmer friend looked serene and pastoral in the afternoon's cloudy but bright conditions. Crows bathed in a puddle in an adjacent meadow. We looked towards North Nibley Monument and it hardly seemed that much could have changed in years. Fortunately, we could neither see nor hear the M5 motorway as it headed north towards Michael Wood service area.

What was clear is that the line of sight towards the site of the one-time Rangeworthy signalbox had all too obviously become obscured by hedges growing up at the lineside. 'No good for photography now,' said George. We moved on to the next overbridge north, a painted inscription on which informed us that it was at 116 miles 36 chains. There was a mature tree on the up (west) side which would scupper the chance of a possible picture of a train; conversely, on the down side of the line George told me that a large and picturesque elm had been lost to Dutch Elm disease. The saplings that had tried to establish themselves in its place had shrivelled and were dying.

In a quarter of an hour or so, no trains had appeared, but suddenly a Virgin Class 47 diesel and train on a CrossCountry service emerged from Wickwar Tunnel. The small trees that had established themselves in the cutting sides leading to the tunnel would have precluded the opportunity for a worthwhile picture. 'I didn't realise that there were still loco-hauled expresses on this route', George comments. 'Thought there were only HSTs.'

We drove on to Chipping Sodbury, past the village and to the common, and negotiated a track to an overbridge which in one direction provided a view of the station area, and in the other along the cutting to the tunnel-mouth. High above the tunnel is a spur of the Cotswolds which had enforced its construction and nearer at hand is the village of Old Sodbury. 'I used to come to Chipping Sodbury in steam days to photograph either the 3.55pm or 5.55pm down South Wales expresses, or else the up "South Wales Pullman". But the sun tended to be head-on for much of the year so that there were just a few occasions when conditions were satisfactory.'

We looked westwards. Chipping Sodbury station was closed in 1962. Its layout was similar to that of Badminton, with loops alongside the platforms, through lines and a footbridge. Once so apparently substantial, all the station buildings have vanished, but there is a loop line on the up side. The goods shed remains intact, and the railway cottages have survived. Sadly, the surroundings have suffered from a general intrusion of wind-borne litter.

There is the noise of approaching train and out from the tunnel comes a General Motors Class 66 diesel locomotive at the head of empty high-capacity coal wagons. The train passes at speed. No chance of a locomotive built at Swindon, nor even of a main line diesel built in Britain, for the Class 66 has been imported from Canada, and is operated by English Welsh & Scottish Railway, a train operating company controlled from the USA.

The cutting sides leading to the tunnel were once lined only with grass which no doubt used to be burnt off regularly each summer by the lengthmen. These days the grass is undisturbed, coarse and tufty. Saplings have taken hold, particularly in the vicinity of the tunnel portal. Part of the cutting-side has slipped. The platelayers' huts and telegraph poles have long gone. The tunnel itself has been notoriously wet and in recent years has had to be closed on account of flooding.

Our short excursion had helped to highlight what has changed in the railway world over the last quarter-century, at least in terms of photography. Then again, new generation railway cameramen or women might be looking for something different.

Painting — it all Comes from Here!

Although George started painting in the 1940s, he had produced only a handful of paintings before the late 1950s. One notable survivor from this early period is one in his collection of a 'Royal Scot' at the head of a retreating train. The chosen location is near Wickwar. He is critical of this 1951 work. 'The sky is too dark and all the vegetation is much too green! If I had painted it in more recent years I would have painted the grass in much yellower colours. There is always dried grass in the countryside. I sent the painting to British Railways with the suggestion that they might like to consider it for the basis of a poster. They turned it down. They said that the wrong engine was at the front of the train — no 'Royal Scots' regularly worked over the Birmingham-Bristol line!'

The next significant painting proved to be a real winner. The marvellous 1956 panned photograph of a 'Britannia' at Westerleigh has been mentioned already. A year or so later, he used it as a basis of a water-colour but the engine depicted was the class-leader, No 70000 *Britannia*, which so far had spent its working life on the Great Eastern section, hauling express trains from London's Liverpool Street station. Early in 1958, the Eastern Region of BR loosened up its style of management and devolved its operations in the Eastern Counties to the Great Eastern Line whose managers proved very successful in putting a distinctive stamp on their activities as they energetically promoted the modernisation of and improvements to railway services.

April 1958 found the Great Eastern Line running a special train to publicise the arrival of the first of its 'English Electric' Type 4 diesels and the detailed report that appeared in *Trains Illustrated* for June 1958 made use of the *Britannia* painting, at a time when the journal was experimenting with the use of colour plates in an otherwise mono production. *TI* featured *Britannia* opposite a half-tone of the first of the new diesels, the captions having the heading of 'The Rivals'. The two types of locomotive were very well matched when it came to performance and

worked turn and turn about on GE Line express trains until 1961, after which the diesels were all-conquering.

What makes George's painting of No 70000 *Britannia* so effective is that the engine really looks as though it is speeding along a main line in the Eastern Counties. Having travelled over the A12 trunk road into Essex that for some way runs parallel to the Colchester main line at the time the 'Britannias' were at work, I can say that the painting

captures the spirit of these engines perfectly. The locomotive is presentably clean but realistically work-stained, a Heiron trademark that represents his craftsmanship. The caption to the reproduction simply reads, 'An impression of the prototype "Britannia" 4-6-2 No 70000 *Britannia* at speed, from a painting by George Heiron'. Actually, although the painting itself was signed, the magazine's caption-writer invented a new artist by wrongly crediting a 'George *G.* Heiron'.

By the time it had been used for *The Majesty of British Steam* in the early 1970s, George's impressive picture of No 70000 *Britannia* had made at least three appearances in print. This reproduction comes from *Majesty of British Steam*.

Looking at the wooden and garishly liveried locomotives that formed the subjects of some of the other *Trains Illustrated* paintings during 1958, I wondered at the sort of reception George's greatly superior study of *Britannia* had received from the publisher. In those days, the Ian Allan Ltd headquarters offices were at Craven House, Hampton Court, a stone's throw from Hampton Court Palace. Craven House very much still remains. It is an 18th century listed building, with Bushy Park at its rear. Company lore has its that office staff enjoyed a daily routine of feeding the park deer with tidbits.

George took his painting to Craven House, and asked at the reception for editorial staff member, Geoffrey Kichenside. That worthy took the unwrapped *Britannia* from George, drew breath, held the painting gingerly by its edges and ran upstairs to Freeman's office, gazing fixedly at what he was holding. The painting had made its mark all right! It was not long before it appeared as a reproduction in another Ian Allan publication where it was accompanied by two other George Heiron paintings.

From the late 1940s the publisher had produced an Ian Allan *Trains Annual*, which aimed to meet the demand for Christmas-time annuals that were principally published for sale as presents to children and sold primarily through W. H. Smith shops. By the 1950s, the attraction of the annuals had grown, not least because Book Tokens had been recently introduced so that Aunt Agatha's thoughtful Christmas present for young Peter was soon used to buy reading matter for the Christmas holidays.

Trains Annual was hardly either a children's picture or a story book and followed much of the content of the monthly *Trains Illustrated*. However, it was considered that its jacket should be eye-catching enough to draw potential purchasers away from the rival delights of, for instance, the *Daily Mail Children's Annual*. In meeting the booksellers' requirements for the Christmas market the annuals had to be ready to go on sale by mid-year. Ian Allan Ltd later refined its appeal to this market by going for three titles — *Trains Annual* became the *Trains Illustrated Annual* so as to anchor it more firmly to the success of the magazine; there was a *Locospotters' Annual* (for schoolboys who were members of the Locospotters' Club); and for the 'youngest member of the railway-lover's family'

(according to the publisher's blurb) there was the *Ian Allan Book of Trains*.

The four-colour jacket of the 1959 *Trains Illustrated Annual* (price 10/6 and edited as usual by Freeman Allen) featured a particularly striking painting from George of a 'King' sending up the echoes past Dr Day's Bridge Junction, Bristol, at the head of the up 'Bristolian' express.

Then came the 1960 edition when George's painting used for the jacket was happily repeated as a full-page colour plate inside the annual. There was another new Heiron painting inside the 1960 *Annual*, where it served as the frontispiece. The captions explained that 'The Colour Plates are from paintings by George F. Heiron. The frontispiece shows a WR 'Castle' 4-6-0 in the Cotswolds, storming up Sapperton bank on the 11.45am from Cheltenham Spa to Paddington on a summer's afternoon. The plate facing page 33 (this was of course the subject of the book jacket) shows 'Britannia' No 70029 *Shooting Star* bringing the up 'Red Dragon' through Badminton, at the summit of the climb from the Severn Tunnel.'

Publishers being frugal folk, *Trains Illustrated Annual 1960* also included colour reproductions that were enjoying a second airing, by virtue of reusing blocks that had been made in the first place for the jackets of Ian Allan books of the last few years. The Heirons were entirely new, but it is worth mentioning that the study of the 'Castle' on Sapperton also enjoyed an encore, as the cover illustration for a small saddle-stitched book on the Great Western.

Following their marriage in 1959, George and Shirley went on holiday to Ilfracombe. George recalls: 'I painted seascapes while we were there and sold them locally. It paid for the holiday. Of course, I also enjoyed photographing trains on that steep incline out of the station.'

This was the period that established George as a painter of railway subjects. He prefers working with water-colours and uses board rather than cartridge paper where there is always the hazard that it will become too wet and cockle up. He comments: 'I like working with the paint always fairly thick on the brush, almost as if I was using oils. I always use the best paints available - in my book that's Winsor & Newton. Water colours are much better when it comes to getting the sort of fine detail that's needed in railway subjects: rivets, pipework, lining-out, the hinges on rolling stock — all that sort of thing.'

'As for references, I only use photographs as a basis, to make sure I get the details right. I always take great trouble with the permanent way — track, sleepers and fastenings and the ballast. I think it's essential to the impact of the paintings — if the

The jacket for the 1959 *Trains Illustrated Annual*.

The 'Castle' on Sapperton bank which made its debut in print in the 1960 *Trains Illustrated Annual*.

track looks wrong, the rest of the subject is affected.'

'Ever since the age of five or six, I have spent so much time on and alongside the railway that I can visualise scenes — it's been a lifelong study, you might say. Everything I have seen has become implanted in my mind's eye. That's the difference, I think, as compared with younger artists who never saw the steam railway at first-hand. They tend to hide up wheels and motion with steam. Very often the coupling and connecting rods are completely wrong. I must admit though that locomotive driving wheels are difficult to paint because there's always the risk of making them too round. The other challenge is to make smoke look like smoke. Some artists seem to portray it flowing like water. Some also make the steam look too dense — it's only water vapour — they seem to forget that.'

'One aspect of painting locomotives has always worried me and that is the appearance of their paintwork. Vic Welch, who painted for Ian Allan Ltd during the time he worked in their studio, portrayed all his locomotives as if they were just out of the paintshop. They look as if they have had buckets of water poured over them. I've tried to paint locomotives to show the effects of travel-staining. Steam locomotives in everyday service always had streaks of dirt; they were never that clean unless they were just ex-works. In my experience, they always had an oily look, the result of engine cleaners using paraffin and rags when cleaning them on shed. I've never painted engines with bright-red buffer beams — they were never like that! After a short time in traffic, oil and dirt had accumulated around the rivets. When engines had been in traffic for some time the red faded and almost became pink. Brasswork and copperwork were always somewhat tarnished. After all, engines weren't toys, and they look too good to be true when they're shown as if they have just left the main works.'

'It's the same with rolling stock, particularly coaches. The cream paintwork of Great Western coaches or of the BR blood and custard livery soon became grimy. Trains passed over water-troughs and were stained by smoke and coal dust so it was inevitable that the coaches' exterior condition deteriorated, particularly the roofs. When I'm painting rolling stock I rub a smudge of soot over them to get the correct effect as I remember it.'

'Although my preference is for water-colours, I have worked extensively in oils. You have to know how to handle the medium. I use the same basic techniques as when I'm using water-colours, but you have to paint the detail when the surface of the painting is wet.'

George Heiron's largest single commission for railway paintings came in the early 1970s. Freeman Allen asked him to take on what the publisher described in its publicity as 'the most handsome and colourful tribute to the British steam locomotive yet published'. The book was to landscape format, to an 11¾in x 9in in page size and heavy art paper was used throughout. The book was entitled *The Majesty of British Steam* and went on sale in 1973. O. S. Nock, the renowned writer on railways generally and steam locomotives in particular, contributed an introductory essay that outlined British steam locomotive development, at the same time providing something of a commentary on the subjects of the paintings.

The idea was that within a range of over 40 paintings, all but two of which were specially produced for *The Majesty of British Steam*, the book would feature representative British steam locomotive designs of the late 19th and 20th centuries, from colourful pre-Grouping Singles, to 4-4-0s and Atlantics, and from the big 4-6-0s and Pacifics of the Big Four, to the postwar classes. BR Standard designs were represented by that 1958 painting of *Britannia* at speed!

The Majesty of British Steam was something of a tall order for George. 'The book was certainly the first of its kind and Ian Allan Ltd was in a hurry to get it in print. Freeman Allen chose the photographs that were to serve as my references and I was sent details of engine and rolling stock liveries. The lighting conditions were left to me. There were 46 paintings to turn out, and I painted day and night to keep to a schedule that required me to produce a painting every week. Freeman became desperate by the time I had got to the last picture which was of an Adams 4-4-2T standing at Waterloo. "Should we leave it out?" he kept saying, but I completed it and the book turned out to be a great success.'

The very last one — George's painting of an Adams 4-4-2T at Waterloo was the last painting of 46 he completed in double-quick time for *The Majesty of-British Steam*.

'Castles' meet on Ashley bank. No 7017 *G. J. Churchward* fills the foreground as a sister engine storms up the bank with the 'Bristolian'. This painting was based on one of George's own photographs.

The subjects of *The Majesty of British Steam* paintings were certainly varied, not just in terms of the locomotive types but in the range of duties the engines were engaged upon, the parts of Britain featured, and indeed the origins of the photographs that Freeman Allen had assembled for George.

There were Wethersett's fine studies from the 1930s, such as of a streamlined 'Princess Coronation' Pacific hastening past Kilburn in north-west London on its way to Glasgow with the LMS 'Coronation Scot' streamliner, or of an ex-Great Northern Atlantic accelerating from Cambridge with

one of the buffet car expresses to King's Cross. Some of the other references came from photographs in the collection of the Locomotive Publishing Co which had been acquired by Ian Allan Ltd in the late 1950s. These served as a basis for George's water colours which as realised portrayed some handsome engines and attractive trains generally, such as a London Tilbury & Southend 4-4-2T energetically on the move through Barking; a Midland & Great Northern Joint Railway 4-4-0 departing from Yarmouth Beach station on a bright summer's day; and a North Staffordshire 4-4-0 making a stately departure from Stoke-on-Trent. One or two of the paintings drew inspiration from Big Four companies' publicity pictures of the 1920s and 1930s.

Two or three of the subjects in *The Majesty of British Steam* made use of George's own photographs that had been reproduced in *Trains Illustrated* and no doubt were favourites of the Editor's. One was the meeting on Ashley Hill bank of a 'Castle' drifting downgrade as a class-member stormed out of Bristol at the head of the 'Bristolian' bound for Paddington. Another was of a 'Hall' 4-6-0 on a biting winter day, pulling steadily up the bank from Stoke Gifford yards with a freight train for the Midlands.

Not only was *The Majesty of British Steam* a success in its own right but over the next decade or so paintings in the selection were chosen for reuse on the jackets of other major titles in the Ian Allan Ltd list. Some were used for the 'At Work' series which included profiles of the life and times of major locomotive types, such as the West Coast and East Coast Pacifics, Stanier Pacifics and 4-6-0s, and the Bulleid Pacifics.

From the mid to late 1970s it was recognised by publishers that four-colour jackets were essential in securing good sales for their book titles. Consequently, it ensured that there would be a steady stream of commissions for George, not least from Ian Allan Ltd. It was an interesting challenge to locate a black and white print from among the collection supplied by an author for his book and then dispatch it to George with an instruction perhaps to change the location, locomotive livery or rolling stock to suit the painting required for the jacket. The editorial and production team involved never ceased to marvel at the way he interpreted their challenge, often providing a new insight into the subject that was based on his own extensive knowledge of the railway scene over the years.

Not all the paintings called for by Ian Allan Ltd were of railway subjects, for the publisher's list included aviation, naval and merchant shipping titles. George's interest and knowledge of aircraft derived from his time with the Bristol Aeroplane Co at Filton and usually the aircraft required to be depicted were World War 2 types.

Two or three of the commissions from Ian Allan Ltd for ship paintings were to provide the subject of jackets for largely pictorial books written by

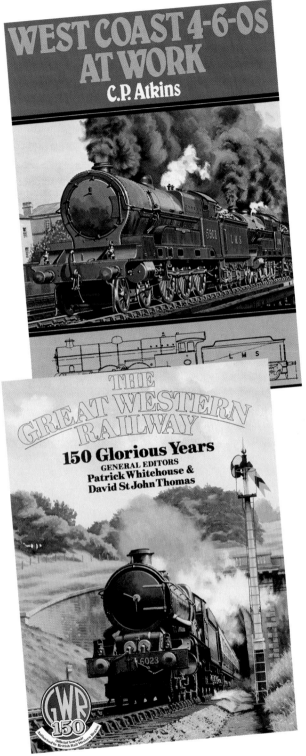

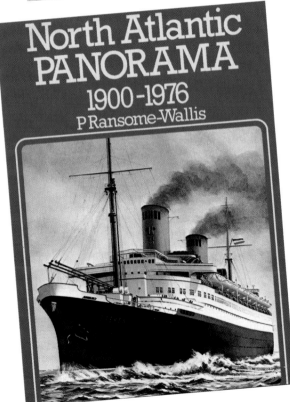

George's fine study of a pair of ex-London & North Western Railway 'Claughton' 4-6-0s getting to grips with Camden bank in LMS days was reused to provide the subject of the jacket for Phil Atkins' *West Coast 4-6-0s at Work*, **an Ian Allan title of 1981.**

The jacket for *The Great Western Railway 150 Glorious Years*, **published by David & Charles.**
Courtesy of David & Charles

Heirons in less expected fields — a painting for *Messerschmitt Bf109 at War* **and for** *North Atlantic Panorama 1900-1976*, **both Ian Allan titles.**

Dr P. Ransome-Wallis and were illustrated using some of the author's own extensive collection of photographs over the last half-century. Typical was George's painting of the 1928-vintage SS *Bremen* that graced the jacket of *North Atlantic Panorama 1900-1976*. I admired George's oil painting of *Cutty Sark* in his own collection, not least on account of the 'glassiness' of the sea, for so often artists render salt water as almost opaque. He commented: 'When I went overseas on National Service we travelled by boat and I spent a lot of time studying the effect of light on the sea, the way that it changed colour in different weather conditions and the relationship between the sky, cloud cover and the sea.'

George had worked hard to produce a painting a week to fulfil the requirement of paintings for *The Majesty of British Steam* but as the number of commissions had steadily increased, his output throughout the 1980s and into the early 1990s ran at a steady rate of a painting a week — without a break.

An unusual painting from this period depicted a railway scene that never was. Music promoter, Yellow Two Productions, decided in 1987 to issue a

'Princess Coronation' class 4-6-2 No 6231 *Duchess of Atholl* seen working hard on the climb up Beattock bank with a Euston-Glasgow express, circa 1939. This oil painting was the first of many commissioned by Barrie Meikle in 1987.
GH: The locomotive actually fills most of the picture entailing a great deal of fine detail work. I positioned the driving rods at the top half of the wheels rather than the bottom as I always think they look more powerful set in this position.

Coronation Scot
and
Reginald Gardiner's
Trains

The sleeve for Yellow Two Productions' long-playing record *Coronation Scot* — a red LMS streamlined Pacific with the set of 1939/40 'Coronation Scot' coaches — a scene that might have been, but wasn't!

long-playing record (LP) that featured music with a railway theme such as Eric Coates's *Coronation Scot*, along with the famous imitations of railway sounds by Reginald Gardiner. The idea was that the record sleeve ought to have an unusual subject and the one chosen was of a streamlined LMS Pacific climbing to Shap Summit with the 1939/40 'Coronation Scot' set of coaches painted in maroon and gold livery. These vehicles never ran in service in this scheme because they were shipped to the United States for the New York World's Fair of 1939 and were marooned overseas until the end of World War 2. The painting for the sleeve therefore represented an intriguing might-have-been.

Paintings for reproduction on LP sleeves were nothing new for George. He had been asked by Peter Handford, sound recordist extraordinaire who had recorded the sounds of our steam railways at work in the 1950s and 1960s, to supply black and white photographs, particularly of trains at night, for use in the design of LP sleeves published during the 1960s under the Argo Transacord label. Later record issues made use of reproductions of George's paintings specially commissioned for the purpose.

Among the railway publishing successes of the mid to late 1980s was a series of large format David & Charles titles beginning with *The Great Western Railway 150 Glorious Years*. This first book was published in 1984 in anticipation of the GWR 150 celebrations the following year. The books were complied under the joint editorship of the late Patrick Whitehouse and David St John Thomas and later titles dealt with Southern 150, LMS 150 and LNER 150.

Pat Whitehouse was an old acquaintance and in his many and varied railway publishing projects had made good use of George's photographs. George was commissioned to produce a painting for the jacket of *The Great Western Railway 150 Glorious Years* and it was a handsome study of a 'King' emerging from Box Tunnel with a Paddington-Bristol express of the 1930s. Fifteen or so of his black and white photographs were used between its covers. The book went on to sell in tens of thousands so George's work must have entered a tremendous number of homes. The final title under the David Thomas/Whitehouse editorship appeared in 1993. This was the *Romance of Scotland's Railways*, published under the Thomas & Lochar imprint. Its jacket and frontispiece were reproduced from George's painting of Kyle of Lochalsh as seen in the late 1930s with an ex-Highland Railway 4-6-0 shunting the yard, a coastal steamer laying a smokescreen over the harbour, and clouds forming over Skye with their ominous implication that the next day might be characteristically damp!

By the time that *Romance of Scotland's Railways* had appeared, George was being commissioned by Brian Stephenson of RAS Publishing to paint a variety of locomotive types that were being featured in issues of the long-running *Locomotives Illustrated* bi-monthly magazine. Many older locomotive types had ceased to turn a wheel before colour photography became commonplace and so it was essential to have an eye-catching painting as the basis of the cover design. Some memorable paintings resulted from this collaboration.

Scope for George's historical railway paintings has increased with the current Ian Allan Publishing series of studies of pre-Grouping railways. Among the latest have been *Furness Railway: A View from the Past* and *Cornish Riviera: A View from the Past*, both having been published in 2000.

With his remarkable output of paintings George is at pains to stress that he has always handled all his own negotiations with purchasers and has never employed an agent. 'I prefer the personal touch and most of the commissions have come from people writing to me — I've regarded them as friends. I've never had a studio — always worked from home — it all comes from here! Mind you, I would have liked a studio in the roof of my house but I have never got round to it.'

He works quickly and without fuss. 'I only use an easel for oil paintings, never for water-colours. Generally, I paint during the afternoons and on into the evenings. One near-disaster sticks in my memory. I was working on a water-colour for Ian Allan Ltd of trains on Camden bank, outside Euston station. I tipped a pot of water over the work when

The 20-coach 'Canadian' traversing the Kicking Horse Pass in the Rockies. It is threading a short rock tunnel at the base of Mount Stephen, in the centre background is Cathedral Crags. This was produced as a rough for a jigsaw.

it was nearly finished. A lot of the painting was stained and it had to be extensively repainted!'

The commissions for paintings have been many and varied. An industrialist in the north-west of England informed George that 'if I have to wait 10 years I want as many paintings as George can paint!' Director of the Dart Valley Railway, John Evans, is another admirer of his work and insists that the paintings must include a representation of Shirley!

Over the years, some of *The Majesty of British Steam* paintings were licensed for reproduction and in time their producers came to George for new subjects which have included European crack trains such as the 'Simplon-Orient Express' and the 'Flèche d'Or'. 'But,' says George, 'I have never made up any of the jigsaws featuring my paintings.' Some of the David & Charles 150 series book jackets were given a less expected exposure when they were adapted for tea towel designs, so you can actually wipe up with a George Heiron.

Shirley and George had greatly enjoyed their trip to Fort William and the West Highland line in 1961 and so George was particularly pleased to be commissioned to provide a painting for the Glenfinnan Station Museum Trust. Its subject was trains crossing at Glenfinnan on the Mallaig Extension line in late LNER days.

David & Charles had recently published *The Great Days of the Country Railway* whose jacket had included a reproduction of George's painting depicting a 'K2' 2-6-0 standing at Glenfinnan station and an approaching passenger train double-headed by a pair of ex-North British 4-4-0s. It had attracted the attention of John Barnes who was engaged in setting up the Glenfinnan Station Museum. 'We couldn't acquire the original used for the book jacket so I decided to commission George to produce a very similar picture that would serve as a centrepiece for the new museum.'

'The painting was done in oils and at 55cm x 76cm

is my largest in size. I took up the framed painting by train,' says George, 'and protected it during the journey by placing it between my seat and the partition of the coach in which I was travelling.'

The painting was unveiled at the opening of the museum on 21 May 1991 and BR InterCity joined in the celebrations by running a steam special from Fort William to Glenfinnan and back. The occasion also marked the 90th anniversary of Glenfinnan station. The painting and another of George's depicting trains at Glenfinnan station in wintertime are available as postcards and greeting cards. The museum itself is most certainly worth visiting.

Glenfinnan Station Museum and London's Heathrow Airport might seem to be poles apart but another of the prestigious commissions George has received was from David Allan, Chairman of Ian Allan Publishing Ltd, for an aviation painting that now hangs in No 1 Executive Lounge at the airport. Another Heiron may be found at Harrow School, and yet another, less surprisingly, at the National Railway Museum.

When you ask George if he has considered staging an exhibition of his work, his answer is that he has never kept a register of the paintings he has completed. He goes on to make the point that as all but very few have been painted to order, without a considerable amount of organisation, combined with goodwill and co-operation on the part of the owners of his paintings, quite simply he would be unable to mount a representative exhibition of his amazing output of the last 40 or so years. Those that appear as reproductions between the covers of this latest Ian Allan book may well be the nearest to a retrospective of his considerable achievements in paint.

As commissioned by the Glenfinnan Station Museum Trust, George's painting of Glenfinnan station in the last couple of years of the LNER, with a green-painted 'K2' 2-6-0 nearest, and a brace of 'Glen' 4-4-0s approaching.

Courtesy of John Barnes of the Glenfinnan Station Museum Trust

WEST HIGHLAND RAILWAY.
NBR   LNER   BR   SCOTRAIL
GLENFINNAN STATION 1901-1991
TUESDAY 21 MAY 1991.
FORT WILLIAM to
GLENFINNAN
AND RETURN
BY SPECIAL STEAM TRAIN
0301   0301

The special ticket issued by BR InterCity in 1991, for travel on the steam special that was run to mark the opening of the Glenfinnan Station Museum and the station's 90th anniversary.

Courtesy of John Barnes of the Glenfinnan Station Museum Trust

GH painting from No 1 Executive Lounge, London Heathrow Airport.
Courtesy of The Guild of Business Travel Agents

George's View of the World — and his Work

He admits to the sense of a world that is lost — and that what has displaced it falls short. To George Heiron, the Britain of the 1950s and 1960s was a better place. 'People dressed smartly, not like today when they all look so scruffy. When Shirley and I travelled up to London by train in the 1960s we dressed up for the occasion. It made a proper day out, and we used to enjoy having breakfast in the restaurant car.'

The railway of the 1950s and 1960s was, he feels, a friendlier place. 'When I used to go out and about photographing, railwaymen used to wave and smile. Nowadays, you're more likely to attract the attention of the British Transport Police.' For those interested in railways, and those who worked on them, railway territory was effectively open house, providing you obeyed the courtesies expected of a visitor. If you visited stations you were just as likely to be invited to take a look round. If you walked up to an engine at a station and took an interest in it, it was not unusual for the crew to invite you to join them on the footplate. More than likely, the resulting conversation would take in the merits of particular engine types, or latest developments on the railway. Passengers arriving at a terminal station very often went up to the enginemen to thank them for a punctual journey. The world has moved on, but it has become neither more friendly nor more inviting.

Our railways have undoubtedly evolved to become a much more mundane operation. Staff may try their hardest, but public displays of aggression towards them and their varied employers have served to make everyone wary. In any case, staff are not encouraged nowadays to share their thoughts with rail travellers.

Refreshment facilities at stations almost entirely comprise take-aways and sandwich kiosks. The days of refreshment rooms with a daily menu of hot meals have long gone. George and I were discussing Bath Spa station. 'I remember the down side platform and very often at about 5.30-6pm I would go to the refreshment room for something to eat.

Shirley Heiron comfortably ensconced in a second-class compartment of a BR standard coach of the 1950s, formed in the 'Red Dragon' which is waiting to leave Paddington, *circa* 1959/60. First stop, Swindon, next stop Badminton!

The lady serving behind the counter had an aristocratic voice and you were served proper tea on a tray. Nowadays, the down platform at the station just seems dead.'

In reviewing George's railway photography I have tried to convey the way in which the railway environment at track level and all around has changed for the worst. That is, from the point of view of someone who knew much of his local rail network intimately. The industry could never have remained so labour-intensive as it had been in the steam age, but it seems regrettable that privatisation has brought greater deterioration in neatness and a widespread incursion of litter and weeds. As a result, the approaches to major stations are often an eyesore, made more unsightly by the all-pervading graffiti.

One feature of George's 'patch', the area to the north-east of Bristol, is the way in which infilling has occurred along main roads and consequently the countryside has been squeezed out. Yate has expanded into something akin to a new town which sits uneasily alongside the still largely unspoiled Chipping Sodbury. Everywhere greatly increased levels of road traffic have degraded the environment, something that is all too obvious in George's home village of Coalpit Heath with its traffic calming schemes and traffic lights. It is no longer a good place for cyclists. George doesn't drive. He chuckles, 'I don't have a computer either.'

George continues to find railways interesting. For 18 months or so now, he has been affected by a mystery illness which has restricted his mobility so that he can no longer use his bike. But from time to time he and Shirley go out to watch the High Speed Trains tearing along the South Wales main line. Many of his pictures of the late 1970s and 1980s of diesel-hauled trains will become classics in the same way as his images of steam operations. I was reminded of that when choosing some of his prints for a book of mine on the passenger rolling stock of the InterCity period. I admired his clever use of scenery and railway infrastructure such as bridges, retaining walls and viaducts to strengthen the compositions and so put the trains themselves into an interesting context.

I was reminded of what he wrote in the 1970s: 'Railway photography is still a pleasant way of escape from the stress and strain of the workaday world, "up the line" deep in the countryside armed with camera, some tasty sandwiches and a flask of tea. It is a form of relaxation that is enjoyable to me.'

Perhaps, I said to him, he had preferred being self-employed for most of his life - with his ability to mix more mundane assignments with painting for pleasure and his railway photographic activities. He reflected on what I had suggested. 'It was not so much a living — just a simple life, just a pleasure. I loved it — I was a free man.' That seems to sum up George Heiron admirably.

Not quite in steam days, it's true, yet Bath Spa station's Platform 2 looks trim in this late 1960s view.

Modern traction, late 1970s. It's August 1978 and before long HSTs will displace the 'Deltics' such as No 55013 _The Black Watch_ which is waiting at Edinburgh Waverley with the 11.10 to King's Cross.

Gallery

Out towards Rannoch Moor ....

BR Standard '5' 4-6-0 No 73078 and a Stanier 'Black Five' combine to cause echoes to rebound from the boulders of
Monessie Gorge as they head towards Rannoch Moor with the afternoon Fort William-Glasgow Queen St train that
includes through sleeping cars for London King's Cross. A March 1961 photograph.

Out across Rannoch Moor ....

The afternoon Fort William-Glasgow Queen St train approaches one of the typical West Highland Line viaducts on an
afternoon in March 1961.

Badminton in the snow

Daytime - the up 'Red Dragon' passes the station on what George describes as 'a crusty white morning in January 1952'. The engine is No 4091 *Dudley Castle*.

It was a bitter night in January 1958 when George photographed the down 'Red Dragon' as the express made its Badminton stop, with 'Britannia' Pacific No 70029 *Shooting Star* at its head.

Trains in the landscape

Up the 1 in 60 gradient between Chalford and Sapperton No 5980 *Dingley Hall* lays a trail of white smoke among the leafless trees of the Golden Valley. The train is the 2.10pm Cheltenham St James-Swindon stopping train, photographed in February 1956.

Some of the grandeur of the South Wales Direct line is conveyed in this June 1958 study of the Paddington-bound 'Capitals United Express' crossing Winterbourne Viaduct. The train is being hauled by a 'Castle' 4-6-0.

Golden Valley charm:

No 5040 *Stokesay Castle*, a London engine working home, pounds up the 1 in 74 gradient east of Chalford towards Sapperton Tunnel with the 4pm Cheltenham St James-Paddington express of 7 May 1955.

Back in 1953, the young ladies of Brimscombe keep their eyes on a Gloucester Central-Chalford auto-train.

Great Western heyday — 1

A '47xx' 2-8-0 storms up a snow-laden Dainton bank (between Newton Abbot and Totnes) with a westbound heavy
freight in the mid-1930s.

Great Western heyday — 2

One of Ian Allan's favourite paintings! Bristol Temple Meads station in 1936, with an express for London Paddington
headed by 'Castle' 4-6-0 No 100 A1 *Lloyd's*.

Memories of the Baltic tanks — 1

In Midland Railway livery, a Whitelegg 4-6-4T ordered by the London Tilbury & Southend Railway stands in the engine yard at London St Pancras station, circa 1919.

Memories of the Baltic tanks — 2

Hughes 4-6-4T, LMS No 11111, leaves Wigan Wallgate station with a Rochdale-Southport fast train, circa 1930.

Elegant engines

Highland Railway Jones Goods 4-6-0 No 103 was restored to pre-Grouping condition and returned to steam in the late 1950s/early 1960s. It is seen on the Highland section with an enthusiasts' special of that time.

Great Western Railway Dean Single No 3040 *Empress of India* speeds along the main line near Acton at the head of a special working, comprising a carriage truck loaded with road carriage and brake coach, no doubt put on for some well-heeled travellers.

Postwar Pacifics

In its original air-smoothed form 'Merchant Navy' Pacific No 21C5 *Canadian Pacific* heads out of Salisbury with a
Waterloo-West of England express in 1947.

Seen in original condition with handrails on the smoke deflectors, Western Region 'Britannia' Pacific No 70018
Flying Dutchman reposes on shed in the early 1950s.

Apple-green express power

Gresley 'A1' Pacific No 2558 *Tracery* leans into the curve as it departs from Grantham with a King's Cross-Leeds express, circa 1933.

Bound for Harwich Parkeston Quay, the daily cross-country express from Liverpool Central station climbs through the Pennines near Torside behind 'B17' 4-6-0 No 2862 *Manchester United*. This engine will work the train as far as Ipswich.

Britain's independent railways

A scene from the Bishop's Castle Railway which closed in 1935. The engine is 0-6-0 *Carlisle* which was built in 1868 and acquired by the BCR in 1895.

On the Kent & East Sussex Railway, 'Terrier' 0-6-0T No 3 *Bodiam* fusses up to a wayside halt, *circa* 1936.

LMS 4-6-0s on the move — 1

In 1947, the 7.20pm Bristol Temple Meads-Newcastle Mail is seen under a full moon as it at speeds through Yate station behind 'Jubilee' 4-6-0 No 5626 *Seychelles*. The station was close to George's home and he remembers the spectacle as if were only yesterday!

LMS 4-6-0s on the move — 2

No 6125 *3rd Carabinier* was one of the first 'Royal Scot' 4-6-0s to be rebuilt with a taper boiler. In this 1947 scene it is
seen hard at work along the Settle & Carlisle line with the 3.40pm Bradford Forster Square-Carlisle train.
GH: This was an action study of a locomotive at speed.

Cambrian passenger trains

Pre-Grouping years: Cambrian Railways 4-4-0 No 50, built 1891, leaves Harlech with an up passenger train in July 1911.

GWR years: the 1pm Aberystwyth-Whitchurch of August 1938, making the ascent of Talerddig bank behind the combination of GWR '32xx' 4-4-0 No 3203 and ex-Cambrian Railways Jones Goods, GWR No 844.

Waverley departures

From the east end of Edinburgh Waverley, the up 'Queen of Scots' Pullman train sets out for Leeds and London King's Cross in July 1932 behind ex-North Eastern Railway Raven Pacific No 2401 *City of Kingston upon Hull*.

A scene from over 20 years later of Peppercorn 'A1' Pacific No 60152 *Holyrood* setting out from the west end of the station with an express for Aberdeen.

Night stars

In unrebuilt form 'Royal Scot' 4-6-0 No 6135 *The East Lancashire Regiment* climbs Beattock on a moonlit night in the late 1930s with a down West Coast postal train.

That evening stop at Badminton station: the down 'Red Dragon sets out for South Wales and beyond behind 'Britannia' 4-6-2 No 70028 R*oyal Star* on a cold night in the late 1950s. This painting was used on the jacket of George Heiron's book *Trains to the West*.

Pre-Grouping engines on the Southern — 1

Under ac overhead electrification, ex-London Brighton & South Coast Railway 'E4' 0-6-2T No B473 (formerly named
Birch Grove and now preserved on the Bluebell Railway) arrives at East Croydon with a suburban train from
London Bridge, circa 1925.

Pre-Grouping engines on the Southern — 2

Ex-South Eastern & Chatham Railway rebuilt Stirling 'F1' 4-4-0 No 1078 arrives at Charing with a London Victoria-Maidstone East-Ashford stopping train, circa 1937.

Original and modified 'Kings'

King class 4-6-0 No 6009 *King Charles II* seen passing Stapleton Road junction with the up 'Bristolian' in the mid-1950s.

In the early 1960s some 'Kings', by now fitted with double chimneys and other improvements, took over some duties on the Paddington-South Wales service. No 6016 *King Edward V* makes a fine sight with the eastbound 'Red Dragon' express.

LMS Pacifics taking a pause — 1

The unique turbine-driven No 6202 'Turbomotive' at the head of a Liverpool express, circa 1937.

LMS Pacifics taking a pause — 2

An early 1950s' study of 'Princess Coronation' No 46239 *City of Chester* on Crewe North shed. George considers this to be one of his best 'Duchess' paintings, alive with smoke, steam and men. He comments 'one can hear the roar of the safety valves, the rumble of boiler pressure and the clink of long narrow shovels'.

Freight trains of long ago — 1

Midland & South Western Junction Railway 2-6-0 No 16 (nicknamed 'Galloping Alice') heads south along the cross-country line, circa 1917, with a train of battle-tanks for shipping to the Western Front. This engine spent just a short time painted in this green livery.

Freight trains of long ago — 2

Down from Shap Summit comes a southbound West Coast freight in 1928. The engine is the first (and subsequently preserved) London & North Western Railway design 'G2' class 0-8-0, LMS No 9395.

Peppercorn Pacifics — 1

Destined to be the last survivor of the 49 members of the 'A1' class, No 60145 *Saint Mungo* is seen north of the border
at the head of the 'Flying Scotsman' express.

Peppercorn Pacifics — 2

The first of the Peppercorn 'A2s' was No 525 *A. H. Peppercorn*, seen departing London King's Cross station with an express, soon after it was built in late 1947.

Streamliner glory days — 1

Double-chimney 'A4' 4-6-2 No 4902 *Seagull* at King's Cross Top Shed during the all too brief 15 months between the
engine's entry to service and the outbreak of World War 2.

Streamliner glory days — 2

Crewe North shed in 1938, with brand-new, red-liveried 'Princess Coronation' Pacific No 6226 *Duchess of Norfolk*
and one of the first five of the class completed the previous year in blue and silver livery.
GH: I visualised two streamlined Pacifics standing side-by-side outside the shed.

North Eastern engines — 1

Soon to be rebuilt as a 4-6-2T, a Raven 'H1' class 4-4-4T, LNER No 2144, departs from Newcastle Central with an up
stopping train in August 1932.

North Eastern engines — 2

North Eastern Railway No 901, the first of five 'T3' 0-8-0s. It is seen passing Cowton, on the Darlington-York main line, with an up goods train in 1920.

LMS freight action — 1

Fowler 2-6-4T No 2397 (one of the 30 engines of this type with side-window cabs) works hard assisting a northbound
freight which is making the ascent through the Westmorland fells from Tebay to Shap.

LMS freight action — 2

With a lengthy train of private owner wagons loaded with coal, '8F' 2-8-0 No 8072 takes the Melton Mowbray line
out of Nottingham. George comments 'my Hornby Dublo "8F" is not as powerful as this, as it can only handle
40 covered wagons!'

Southern heyday

Based on a Southern Railway publicity photograph of 1931, this painting depicts a scene at Seaton Junction with the main section of the 'Atlantic Coast Express' from Waterloo speeding through behind 'King Arthur' 4-6-0 No 455 *Sir Launcelot*. On the up side of the line an 'S15' 4-6-0 No 824 pauses in-between shunting, and nearest is the branch train for Seaton worked by an ex-LBSCR 'D1' 0-4-2T.

Headed by 'Schools' 4-4-0 No 909 *St Paul's*, a Charing Cross-Kent Coast express of the 1930s makes the stop at Waterloo. Combine Ian Allan's favourite class of Southern Railway locomotive, the location of his first paid employment and George's skill with the paint brush and you end up with the jacket painting for *Driven by Steam*.

Bulleid Pacifics at Work

'Battle of Britain' No 21C155 *Fighter Pilot* at the west end of Salisbury station, about to depart with the daily Plymouth-Brighton express in the summer of 1947. This painting was based on one of George's photographs taken on one of his cycle rides to Salisbury.

Headed by rebuilt 'Merchant Navy' Pacific No 35023 *Holland-Afrika Line*, the up 'Atlantic Coast Express' of the early 1960s emerges from the east end of Buckhorn Weston Tunnel, west of Gillingham, Dorset. Note the abrupt change of gradient - the train is picking up speed down the 1 in 100 towards Gillingham.

Steam up!

Gresley 'A3' Pacific No 60093 *Coronach* was withdrawn in April 1962. One of her last duties was to work a Carlisle-Darlington football special, with which *Coronach* is seen leaving Carlisle, to take the Tyne Valley line via Hexham.

One of George's favourite paintings! Working hard up the steep climb out of Bath Green Park station and towards Combe Down Tunnel are LMS '2P' 4-4-0 No 563 and Stanier 'Black Five' 4-6-0 No 4804, bound for Bournemouth over the Somerset & Dorset line.

South Western stalwarts

A scene along the main line between Woking and Basingstoke in pre-Grouping days of '700' class 0-6-0 (nearest) on a down special train, about to be overtaken by Adams 'T6' 4-4-0 No 678, leading engine on a double-headed express.

The now preserved Drummond 'M7' 0-4-4T No 30053 approaches Corfe Castle station with a Wareham-Swanage push-pull train of the 1950s.

Railways abroad — 1

This powerful scene of the interwar 'Orient Express', seen on the Italian side of the Simplon Tunnel was produced for
a jigsaw marketed by Falcon Games.

Railways abroad — 2

Two massive 'T1b' 'Selkirk' 2-10-4 locomotives heave the eastbound 'Dominion' of the Canadian Pacific Railway up
the 1 in 45 gradient of the 'Big Hill' towards the 5,335ft altitude of the great Divide, in the Rocky Mountains.
George painted this scene as a rough for a jigsaw.

Contrasting British expresses of the 1930s — 1

Much of the pre-Grouping atmosphere of Britain's railways survived little changed into the 1930s. In 1932,
ex-Great Central Railway 'D10' 4-4-0 No 5434 *The Earl of Kerry* enters Nottingham Victoria station with the 2.20pm
Manchester London Road-London Marylebone express.

Contrasting British expresses of the 1930s — 2

A final glimpse of the streamliner age: the southbound 'Coronation Scot' on its 6½hour run from Glasgow Central-
London Euston descends Shap at 100mph behind blue-liveried 'Princess Coronation' Pacific No 6221 *Queen Elizabeth*.
A 1937 scene. George was particularly pleased with this painting.

Index